All About Animals
Wolves

By Christina Wilsdon

Reader's Digest Young Families

Contents

Chapter 1

Wolf Pups Grow Up

A pack of gray wolves huddle together on a cold morning in early spring. Their warm breath makes clouds in the chilly air. But just a few feet away, one wolf is snug and warm in a den underground. Her furry body curls around five newborn pups. Each fuzzy brown pup is just 6 inches long—about the length of a dollar bill.

The tiny pups squirm and whimper. They can't see, because their eyes are still tightly shut. They can't hear or walk yet, either. They can only creep by pulling themselves along with their front legs.

Scrabbling and shoving, the pups snuggle against their mother. Then they settle down as they drink her warm milk.

The mother wolf will live in the den with her pups for almost a month. She will step outside only to pass waste and to drink water. Her mate and the other wolves in the pack will hunt and bring her food.

Growing Pups

A wolf pup weighs about one pound when born. It gains two to three pounds a week during the first 14 weeks of its life.

Two weeks go by. The pups open their eyes, which are blue. They can walk now, and their baby teeth are growing. When they are three weeks old, the pups leave the den for the first time. The rest of the pack greets them eagerly. They sniff the pups from nose to tail. The pups jump at the big wolves, pawing them and licking their faces.

All the wolves in the pack help care for the pups. They guard them as they play outside the den. A grown-up wolf even baby-sits if the mother goes hunting with the pack.

The wolves all help feed the pups, too. They carry food in their stomachs to the pups. When the pups lick and nuzzle a wolf's mouth, it coughs up the food for them.

By the time the pups are nine weeks old, they stop drinking milk and eat only meat. They look more like adult wolves now, but their heads and feet are still too big for their bodies. Their coats are a mixture of puppy fuzz and adult hair.

Baby Blues

A wolf cub's blue eyes turn yellow by the time it is four months old.

Baby Teeth

Wolf pups lose their baby teeth, just like human children do! Their permanent teeth have grown in by the time the pups are six months old and ready to hunt with the pack.

The pups' world is limited to the area outside their den for their first weeks of life. But they find lots to do! The chubby little wolves chase mice and chew sticks. They wrestle and romp. They climb on adult wolves that are trying to nap and bite their tails!

When the pups are a little older, their world grows a bit bigger. They travel with the pack to a new area called a rendezvous site. Now the pups can explore an even bigger area. For the next few weeks, this site will be the pack's meeting place. Then they will all move to a different rendezvous site.

By the time the pups are six months old, they are nearly as big as adult wolves. They are strong enough to learn the hunting skills they need to survive.

Their first winter is harsh and cold, but deer are plentiful. The pups eat well and grow stronger. In spring, the year-old pups are fully grown at last. Now they help bring food to their mother as she raises a new litter in the old den.

Home Wolf or Lone Wolf?

A wolf has a decision to make when it grows up. It can stay with the pack and help raise its younger brothers and sisters. Or it can leave when it is about two years old and find a mate. A wolf that leaves the pack also leaves the pack's territory. It strikes out to find a new home of its own.

Chapter 2
The Body of a Wolf

A wolf's paw can be up to 5 1/2 inches long. Tough pads and long claws help the wolf climb rocks and grip the ground when it runs.

Wild Dogs

What furry animal wags its tail, loves to play, and howls? You would be right if you guessed either "wolf" or "dog." The wolf is the ancestor of all dogs. Some dogs, such as huskies, look a lot like wolves. Other dogs, like poodles, don't.

Gray wolves are the biggest wild dogs. A large male wolf can be 6 feet long from nose to tail. Stand a yardstick next to his shoulder, and he may be just as tall as it is!

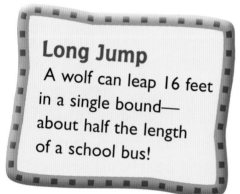

Long Jump
A wolf can leap 16 feet in a single bound—about half the length of a school bus!

Much of this height comes from a wolf's legs. Long legs are good for running. Scientists have recorded wolves sprinting at speeds up to 30 miles per hour—about as fast as a car on a city street.

A wolf can run at top speed only for a little while. But it can trot for many hours at 5 miles per hour—about as fast as a person walking briskly. It can also lope at 20 miles per hour for about 20 minutes while chasing prey. That's about as fast as a person running.

Why does a wolf need to be a good runner? Because it eats deer, moose, and caribou—animals that run even faster!

Wolf Senses

A wolf uses its sharp senses to find food. Its sense of smell is especially keen. Wolves can smell other animals from a distance of about 300 yards—nearly the length of three football fields. One scientist watched a pack of wolves catch the scent of moose that were one-and-a-half miles away! That's about 30 city blocks!

A wolf also has excellent hearing. It can hear a wolf that is howling several miles away. Each ear can swivel in different directions to locate the source of a sound.

A wolf's eyes are good at spotting movement and seeing in low light. This helps the wolf to hunt at dawn, dusk, and at night. But a wolf's eyes are not able to pick out details.

The eyes of a wolf are positioned toward the front of its head, like ours. This helps the wolf judge distances. A deer, on the other hand, has its eyes on the sides of its head. This helps it see nearly all around without even moving its head. Eyes like these help the deer watch out for danger—such as a hungry wolf stalking it!

My, What Big Teeth You Have....

Wolves are carnivores—meat eaters. Like all carnivores, adult wolves have strong, sharp teeth. They can cut through a thick rope with one bite! An adult wolf has 42 teeth. Four are sharp fangs for holding on to prey.

Wolves are lucky to have sensitive ears and noses to help them find food, because their eyesight is not very sharp.

Pups in the same litter sometimes grow adult coats that are different colors.

Coat of Many Colors

Gray wolves are not always gray. They can be white, creamy, or black. Their coats can also be shades of brown, tan, and red. Even a gray wolf's "gray" fur is made up of different shades of gray sprinkled with white, brown, and black hairs.

Wolves that live in the far north tend to be lighter in color than wolves farther south. Most of the wolves that live on the snowy Arctic tundra in Canada are white. Those living in Alaska, however, tend to be gray. Wolves in the forests farther south are usually gray or black.

A wolf gets its color from the long, stiff hairs in its coat called "guard hairs." These hairs grow 4 to 5 inches long on its shoulders and back. They work like a raincoat to shed water. Closer to the wolf's skin is a layer of short, fluffy fur that keeps it warm.

Gray wolf pups are born with fuzzy brown or gray coats. They change into their adult colors when they begin to grow guard hairs.

Winter Coat

A wolf's fur is thick enough to protect it from temperatures below freezing. A wolf in a snowstorm stays warm by curling up and tucking its nose between its hind legs, then covering its face with its tail.

Chapter 3
Wolf Packs

People sometimes tell scary stories about huge wolf packs with hundreds of animals. In reality, wolf packs have fewer than 20 wolves. Usually, packs are only 4 to 8 wolves.

Life in the Wild

A wolf can live alone. It can catch small animals, such as mice, rabbits, and beavers. And it can even kill a deer or moose by itself. But a wolf's life is easier and safer if it is part of a pack.

The pack is the wolf's family. It is usually made up of two parents and their young of different ages. Some packs may also include aunts, uncles, cousins, or unrelated wolves.

All the wolves in a pack work together to catch food and take care of the pups. They defend their home, or territory, from other wolves. A pack's territory is where it roams, hunts, and raises its young.

Top Dogs

The leader of the pack is a strong male wolf. He is often called the alpha male. His mate is known as the alpha female. These two alpha wolves are the only pair in the pack that mate and have pups.

The other wolves in the pack obey the alphas. But these other wolves are not equals. Each wolf has its own place in the pack above or below the other wolves. This place is called a rank.

A wolf can only boss around, or dominate, a wolf of lower rank. A ranking system like this is called a dominance order.

Family Life

A dominance order helps wolves get along with one another. Each wolf knows its place, so it is not always squabbling with other wolves to get its way. Instead, the wolves can work together to survive.

Still, wolves in a pack sometimes quarrel. If you watch a pack of wolves, you may see bared teeth and hear snarls and growls. But you will also see wagging tails and friendly licks. This behavior is all part of how wolves communicate.

Wolves use body language to be friendly, too. A grown-up wolf may greet its father by acting like a puppy begging for food. Maybe you have even seen a dog greet a person in this way.

Wolves also "talk" with their tails. A dominant wolf holds its tail high in the air. A low-ranking wolf holds its tail down. Wolves also wag their tails when they're being friendly, just as dogs do.

Let's Play

Has a dog ever bowed down to you with its tail up in the air, wagging furiously? This action is called a play-bow. It means, "Let's play!" Wolves play-bow when they want to have fun, too.

Wolves "talk" to each other
with their faces and bodies.
An angry wolf may bare its
teeth, wrinkle its forehead,
and point its ears forward.

Baby's First Howl

A wolf pup can howl when it is just two weeks old.

Owooo!

Wolves use sounds to communicate. They whimper and squeak to be friendly, and growl when angry. They may bark if excited or alarmed. But wolves are most famous for howling.

A wolf's howl is a low, mournful cry. It rises and falls like a long, slow song. Other wolves often join in. Scientists have found that humans can hear a wolf's howl from 4 miles away. Most likely, a wolf can hear a howl from an even greater distance.

Wolves howl for many reasons. Howling brings the pack together. It helps pack members keep in touch when they are separated. Howling may also remind other packs to stay out of the wolves' territory.

A wolf that is by itself may use a special "lonesome howl" to call its pack.

Sniff!

Have you ever taken a dog for a walk and stopped at almost every tree? Pet dogs use urine to mark territory with their scent to communicate with other dogs. Wolves do, too. This behavior is called scent marking. A wolf may also rub its body on objects and scratch the ground to leave its scent.

Wolves mark trees, rocks, and other objects in their territory. These scent marks mean "No trespassing!" If a strange wolf wanders into the territory, a few sniffs will warn it to leave. Scent marking may be a way of "building fences" between the territories of different packs.

Chapter 4
Hungry as a Wolf

A pack of wolves on the chase looks ferocious, but the wolves will give up after running a few miles. They may also give up if an animal fights back. Then the wolves go off to find easier prey.

Teamwork

Wolves in a pack work as a team to hunt large animals, such as moose, deer, elk, wild sheep, and bison. Arctic wolves also hunt caribou and musk-oxen.

Wolves find prey as they travel across their territory. Sometimes the wolves smell prey before they see it. Then they follow their noses and sneak up on the animals. Other times wolves may see a herd from a hilltop or surprise a sleeping animal.

When wolves get close to their prey, they creep toward it. The prey may not notice the danger until the wolves suddenly rush at it.

Once in a while, however, the prey refuses to run away! A strong moose, for example, may stand and stare at the wolves until they give up!

Most often, wolves attack animals that are young, old, sick, or injured. These are the easiest animals to catch because they are the weakest and cannot keep up with the herd when the wolves are chasing them. But wolves are also strong and fast enough to catch healthy animals.

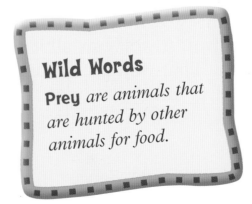

Wild Words

Prey are animals that are hunted by other animals for food.

Time to Eat

Wolves start eating as soon as a kill is made. They tear at the meat with their fangs and "wolf" it down. A hungry wolf can pack 20 pounds of meat into its big, stretchy stomach.

The alpha wolves do not make the other wolves eat after them, as male lions often do. But if the catch is small, such as a moose calf, then the alpha wolves may eat first while the others wait.

Sometimes wolves try to snatch food from one another. But when a wolf has food in its jaws, its rank in the pack does not matter. A young wolf does not have to give its food to an older one. If food is hard to find, however, the parents may boss around the older wolves to make sure the youngest pups are well fed.

After a meal, the pack rests. The wolves need to get their energy back after a chase. Resting also gives their bodies time to digest food. A wolf digests its food quickly, so it may eat again in just a few hours.

Being able to eat this way may seem greedy, but it is useful for wolves. A wolf eats all it can when food is available. That way, it can survive when there is no food. If hunting is poor, a wolf pack may go for two weeks without eating.

The whole wolf pack eats at the same time when the prey is large.

Hungry wolves don't hunt
only big prey, such as deer.
Wolves often eat beavers
and hares. They can even
survive on mice!

A Web of Life

Deer, moose, and other prey are not the only animals in the wolf's world. Wolves also share their habitat with animals that are not prey—including other predators.

In some places, these predators are bears. Most of the time, bears and wolves have nothing to do with one another. But if a bear stumbles across a wolf pack's prey, the wolves usually run away. Then the bear gets a free meal!

Mountain lions and coyotes have a more difficult time with wolves. Scientists recently found that wolves in Montana chase mountain lions away from their meals. Wolves do not get along with coyotes at all and will chase and even kill them.

Bird Games

Ravens seem to have a special bond with wolves. They follow wolves when they see them hunting. The big black birds even fly above wolf trails, looking for wolves. Wolves sometimes seem to play with ravens. The birds tease the wolves into leaping at them, and fly away at the very last second. Then the ravens start the game again!

Chapter 5
Wolves in the World

Scientists and others help persuade people that these wild dogs are not the "big bad wolves" of fairy tales.

Where Wolves Live

☐ The **green** area shows where wolves live today.

Just 200 years ago, many kinds of gray wolves roamed North America. Some lived as far south as Mexico. A different species, the red wolf, lived in the southeastern United States.

Europeans who came to North America in the 1600s feared wolves and offered rewards for killing them. In the 1800s, the killing of wolves increased. By the 1960s, no wolves were left in the lower 48 states except for a few hundred in Minnesota and Michigan.

Today large numbers of gray wolves still live in Alaska and Canada, and some live in parts of the northern United States. Gray wolves also live in parts of Europe and Asia.

The Future of Wolves

Wolves have lost much of their habitat as the human population has grown, but laws now protect them and their homes. Fortunately, wolves are very adaptable. They can live in many habitats—prairies, forests, woods, and tundra—as long as they have enough room to roam and prey to hunt.

Most North American wolves still live in Canada, Alaska, and parts of northern Minnesota, Michigan, and Wisconsin. But now their howls can sometimes be heard in parts of Washington, Idaho, Montana, Wyoming, North Dakota, and South Dakota.

Fast Facts About Gray Wolves

Scientific name	*Canis lupus*
Class	Mammals
Order	Carnivora
Size	Up to 3 feet tall at the shoulder
Weight	Males to 110 pounds
	Females to 90 pounds
Life span	About 10 years in the wild
	About 13 years in captivity
Habitat	Forests, woods, tundra, and plains
Top speed	About 30 miles per hour

The Dog Family

Wolves are part of a scientific family called *Canidae*. This family is made up of about 34 species, which include domestic dogs, wild dogs, wolves, coyotes, and foxes.

Glossary of Wild Words

alpha wolf a wolf that is a leader in its pack

ancestor an animal from whom others are descended

caribou reindeer

carnivore an animal that eats meat

dominance order a system in which some wolves in a pack have a higher rank than other wolves

ferocious fierce, savage

genus a large category of related plants or animals consisting of smaller groups (species) of closely related plants or animals

habitat	the natural environment where an animal or plant lives
litter	a group of pups born at the same time
pack	a family or group of wolves that live together
predator	an animal that hunts and eats other animals to survive
prey	animals that are hunted for food by other animals

rendezvous site	an area used by a pack of wolves with young pups
roam	to wander
species	a group of plants or animals that are the same in many ways
sprinting	running as fast as possible for a short distance
territory	an area defended by a wolf pack
tundra	cold, snowy northern lands that lack forests

Index